First Facts®

FUN SCIENCE

Experiments in
LIGHT (AND)
SOUND

with Toys and Everyday Stuff

BY NATALIE ROMPELLA

Consultant:
Paul Ohmann, PhD
Associate Professor of Physics
University of St. Thomas
St. Paul, Minnesota

CAPSTONE PRESS
a capstone imprint

First Facts are published by Capstone Press,
1710 Roe Crest Drive, North Mankato, Minnesota 56003
www.capstonepub.com

Library of Congress Cataloging-in-Publication Data
Rompella, Natalie, author.
  Experiments in light and sound with toys and everyday stuff / by Natalie Rompella.
    pages cm—(First facts. Fun science)
  Includes bibliographical references and index.
  Summary: "Step-by-step instructions for experiments pertaining to light and sound"—Provided
by publisher.
  Audience: 5–8.
  Audience: K to 3.
  ISBN 978-1-4914-5033-8 (library binding)
  ISBN 978-1-4914-5073-4 (paperback)
  ISBN 978-1-4914-5077-2 (eBook PDF)
1. Light—Experiments—Juvenile literature. 2. Sound—Experiments—Juvenile literature. I. Title. II.
Series: First facts. Fun science.
  QC360.R65 2016
  535.078—dc23   2014044895

Editorial Credits
Alesha Sullivan, editor; Kyle Grenz, designer; Jo Miller, media researcher;
Kathy McColley, production specialist

Photo Credits
Capstone Studio/Karon Dubke except: Shutterstock: Katrina Leigh, cover (rubberbands), koya979,
cover (blocks), MichealJayBerlin, cover (black marker), MNI, cover (colored papers)

Printed in the United States of America.
2230

TABLE OF CONTENTS

TURN YOUR HOME INTO A SCIENCE LAB!

For some science projects you need special equipment and laboratories. But other **experiments** can be done in your own home. You can even use your toys and other everyday things!

experiment—a scientific test to find out how something works

Safety First!

You may need an adult's help for some of these experiments. But most of them can be done on your own. If you have a question about how to do a step safely, be sure to ask an adult. Think safety first!

Fireworks, thunder, glow sticks, and movies all involve light or sound in special ways. Have you ever wondered about how sound and light work around you every day? Get ready to uncover the mysteries of sound and light as you learn about science!

FLIP TO PAGE 20 TO SEE HOW THE SCIENCE WORKS IN EACH EXPERIMENT!

FRIGHT NIGHT

If you step outside in the Sun, you'll see your **shadow** on the ground. You may wonder why your shadow changes shape and length sometimes. Get together with a friend or sibling and have a night of fright while playing around with shadows!

Materials:

flashlight

stuffed animal or action figure

paper

scissors

shadow—the dark shape made when something blocks light

Steps:

1. **Turn off the lights and close any shades or curtains to make a room dark.**

2. **Place a flashlight in front of a stuffed animal or action figure. Move the flashlight closer to and farther away from your toy. What does its shadow look like?**

3. **Use a scissors to cut some shapes out of paper to make scary shadows, such as a wolf or ghost. Shine the light in front of the shapes. Move the flashlight around to try out different shadows. How can you make the shadows the scariest?**

4. **Put on a show for a friend!**

SUN POWER

On a clear, summer day the Sun can get really hot! If you're outside too long, you can even get sunburned. See for yourself that **ultraviolet light** from the Sun reaches Earth's surface.

empty plastic CD case

Materials:

scissors

2 rocks

2 pieces of colored construction paper

sunblock

a small, heavy toy

Tip:

If you can't do this project outside, try attaching the colored paper to a window facing the Sun for a couple of days. Compare the two sides of the paper.

ultraviolet light—an invisible form of light that can cause sunburns

Steps:

1. **Find a spot outside that is in direct sunlight.**

2. **Use scissors to cut one sheet of paper so it fits inside of the CD case. Put a small amount of sunblock on the outside of the CD case.**

3. **Set the CD case and the other piece of paper in the Sun. Weigh the paper down with rocks on the corners. Place the toy in the center of the paper.**

4. **Allow the CD case and paper to sit in the Sun for 2 to 3 hours.**

5. **Remove the toy from the paper. What happened to the paper that wasn't covered by the object?**

6. **Slide the piece of paper out of the CD case. What happened to the part of the paper that wasn't under the sunblock?**

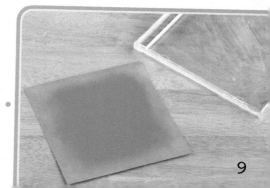

REFLECTION PAINTING

Look closely at your face in a mirror. Does it look the same on both sides of your nose? Have some fun creating a painting in half the time using **reflection** and **symmetry**!

Materials:

white paper

small mirror

full tissue box or stack of books

washable paint

paintbrush

reflect—to bounce off an object

symmetry—the same on both sides of a center line

Steps:

1. Fold a piece of paper in half, open it back up, and set it down on a table.

2. Have an adult help to arrange a mirror so it is standing up along the paper's fold. Use a tissue box or a stack of books to hold the mirror in place.

3. Looking through the mirror, paint one half of a symmetrical shape, such as half of a heart or half of a smiley face.

4. Before the paint dries, fold the paper back over itself, and carefully smooth your hand over where you painted.

5. Open the paper back up and allow it to dry. What does your shape look like?

STAINED-GLASS MASTERPIECE

Light can create beautiful artwork. Stained glass is made up of **translucent**, colored pieces of glass that form a pattern or design. Make your own art with light using some simple kitchen supplies!

Materials:

clear, plastic window found on many pasta boxes and food packaging

aluminum foil

scissors

stapler

hole punch

black permanent marker

washable markers

yarn or string

Beautiful Shapes

Have you ever looked through a toy kaleidoscope? Do you know how it works? It uses light and reflection to repeat an image over and over. Through a kaleidoscope, one small object can look like hundreds!

Steps:

1. Use scissors to cut out the *transparent* window from a pasta box.

2. With a permanent marker, draw the outline of a fish on it. Add an eye and fish scales.

3. Fill in the picture with washable markers, making it colorful. Set aside.

4. Crumple a piece of aluminum foil into a ball. Then smooth it out.

5. Place the foil behind the clear image. Does the aluminum foil make your fish sparkle?

6. Create an ornament by stapling the foil behind the fish image. Cut around the image. Punch a hole in the top, and thread a piece of yarn through it. How is your artwork similar to stained glass?

translucent—letting some light pass through
transparent—easily seen through

SEE THAT SOUND

Can you believe that certain sounds can actually break glass? You may wonder how this is possible. See for yourself with this simple project that allows you to make a bang!

Materials:

small interlocking toy bricks

metal pan

wax paper

small plastic cup or container

permanent marker

toy hammer or large wooden spoon

Tip:
If you can't get the interlocking pieces to move, try something smaller, like grains of rice or small noodles.

rubber band

14

Steps:

1. Make a drum by placing a piece of wax paper over the top of the plastic cup. Secure the wax paper with a rubber band.

2. Set the small interlocking toy bricks onto the drum. Trace around the pieces with a marker.

3. Place the pan and drum side-by-side. Bang on the pan with the toy hammer.

4. Watch what happens to the interlocking pieces. Did they move outside of your traced lines?

15

MUSICAL RUBBER BANDS

Musical ***instruments*** make different sounds and have different ***pitches***. That's why music is so much fun to listen to! Make your own instrument using rubber bands.

Materials:

small container, such as a shoe box

rubber bands of different widths

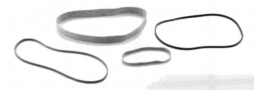

Tip:

If you don't have rubber bands of different widths, try pinching them at different points with one hand. At the same time, pluck with the other hand.

instrument—something used to make music
pitch—how high or low a sound is

Steps:

1. **Place the rubber bands around the container.**

2. **Pull the rubber bands gently, and then let go. Which has a lower pitch—a thicker or thinner rubber band?**

3. **Try making up a new song on your instrument.**

Musical Glasses!

Did you know that your drink can also be an instrument? Fill a couple of drinking glasses with different amounts of water. Gently tap near the top of each glass with the end of a pen or spoon. Which glass made the lowest sound—the one with the most or least amount of water?

BE A FOLEY ARTIST!

Turn on your favorite TV show or movie. Close your eyes and just listen. Can you tell from the sounds what is happening in the scene? People who create these sounds for TV shows and movies are called Foley artists. You can be a Foley artist using toys from your bedroom!

Materials:

comic book or picture book

small toys made out of various materials, such as marbles or small interlocking toy bricks

plastic eggs or other small plastic containers

Steps:

1. **Pick a comic or story that has a lot of action. Try to find things in the story that you can match up with sounds, such as a loud boom, a door slamming, or the rattle of a rattlesnake.**

2. **Use your toys to make noises to fit these scenes. Slide the toys across a hard surface or place them in plastic eggs and shake them. Also try hitting them with your hand. Are you able to make sounds for each scene? Which sounds were the hardest to create? Which were the easiest?**

3. **Share your story and sounds with a friend or sibling.**

WHY IT WORKS

Are you wondering how these amazing experiments worked? Here is the science behind the fun!

PAGE 6 - FRIGHT NIGHT

Solid objects that cannot be seen through, such as a stuffed animal, block light. The shadow will show wherever there is a lack of light. Having the flashlight close to the object will make a large shadow. Having the flashlight farther away from the object will make a smaller shadow. If the flashlight is held in different spots, the shadow will be shortened or stretched.

PAGE 8 - SUN POWER

The toy blocked the Sun's **rays**, keeping the paper underneath it from fading. Sunblock helps block the harmful ultraviolet rays from the Sun. This is why the paper under the sunblock inside the CD case was protected.

PAGE 10 - REFLECTION PAINTING

You drew only half of the shape because light hit the mirror and showed the same image as what was on the paper.

PAGE 12 - STAINED-GLASS MASTERPIECE

The clear plastic is transparent, letting light through it. The permanent marker is **opaque**, and the washable markers are translucent. The aluminum foil bounces light in different directions, making the image sparkle.

PAGE 14 - SEE THAT SOUND

When you hit the pan, it created **vibrations**. The vibrations from banging on the pan traveled through the air to the drum. When the surface of the drum vibrated, the interlocking toy bricks moved.

PAGE 16 - MUSICAL RUBBER BANDS

The thicker the rubber band is, the slower it will vibrate, creating a low sound. The thinner the rubber band is, the quicker it will vibrate, creating higher-pitched sounds.

PAGE 18 - BE A FOLEY ARTIST!

Your toys make different sounds when you play with them, shake them, or hit them against your hand. Some objects vibrate more when they hit one another, making sharper sounds. Others **absorb** the vibrations and make less noise or softer sounds.

ray—a line of light that beams out from something bright
opaque—not letting light through
vibration—a fast movement back and forth
absorb—to soak up

GLOSSARY

absorb (ab-ZORB)—to soak up

experiment (ik-SPEER-uh-muhnt)—a scientific test to find out how something works

instrument (IN-struh-muhnt)—something used to make music

opaque (oh-PAKE)—not letting light through

pitch (PICH)—how high or low a sound is

ray (RAY)—a line of light that beams out from something bright

reflect (ri-FLEKT)—to bounce off an object

shadow (SHAD-oh)—the dark shape made when something blocks light

symmetry (SIM-uh-tree)—the same on both sides of a center line

translucent (transs-LOO-suhnt)—letting some light pass through

transparent (transs-PAIR-uhnt)—easily seen through

ultraviolet light (uhl-truh-VYE-uh-lit LITE)—an invisible form of light that can cause sunburns

vibration (vye-BRAY-shuhn)—a fast movement back and forth

READ MORE

Hall, Pamela. *Listen! Learn About Sound.* Science Definitions. Mankato, Minn.: Child's World, 2011.

Harbo, Christopher L. *What's That Shadow?: A Photo Riddle Book.* Nature Riddles. Mankato, Minn.: Capstone Press, 2010.

Spilsbury, Louise, and Richard Spilsbury. *Why Can't I Hear That?: Pitch and Frequency.* Exploring Sound. Chicago: Heinemann Library, 2014.

INTERNET SITES

FactHound offers a safe, fun way to find Internet sites related to this book. All of the sites on FactHound have been researched by our staff.

Here's all you do:

Visit *www.facthound.com*

Type in this code: 9781491450338

Super-cool stuff!   Check out projects, games and lots more at
www.capstonekids.com

INDEX